HEADLINE SERIES

No. 314   FOREIGN POLICY ASSOCIATION   Spring

The U.S. Role in the Twenty-first Century World:
Toward a New Consensus?

by Stanley R. Sloan

Cover Design: Ed Bohon $5.95

The Author

STANLEY R. SLOAN is the senior specialist in international security policy for the Congressional Research Service, Library of Congress. Before joining CRS, he served as deputy national intelligence officer for Western Europe with the Central Intelligence Agency and was a member of the U.S. delegation to the Vienna talks on East-West troop reductions in 1973. A graduate of the University of Maine with an MIA from Columbia University, Mr. Sloan lectures widely in Europe and the United States. His most recent book is *NATO's Future: Beyond Collective Defense*.

The Foreign Policy Association

The Foreign Policy Association is a private, nonprofit, nonpartisan educational organization. Its purpose is to stimulate wider interest and more effective participation in, and greater understanding of, world affairs among American citizens. Among its activities is the continuous publication, dating from 1935, of the HEADLINE SERIES. The author is responsible for factual accuracy and for the views expressed. FPA itself takes no position on issues of U.S. foreign policy.

HEADLINE SERIES (ISSN 0017-8780) is published four times a year, Spring, Summer, Fall and Winter, by the Foreign Policy Association, Inc., 470 Park Avenue So., New York, NY 10016. Chairman, Paul B. Ford; President, Noel V. Lateef; Editor in Chief, Nancy Hoepli-Phalon; Senior Editors, Ann R. Monjo and K.M. Rohan; Assistant Editor, Nicholas Barratt. Subscription rates, $20.00 for 4 issues; $35.00 for 8 issues; $50.00 for 12 issues. Single copy price $5.95; double issue $11.25. Discount 25% on 10 to 99 copies; 30% on 100 to 499; 35% on 500 and over. Payment must accompany all orders. Postage and handling: $2.50 for first copy; $.50 each additional copy. Second-class postage paid at New York, N.Y., and additional mailing offices. POSTMASTER: Send address changes to HEADLINE SERIES, Foreign Policy Association, 470 Park Avenue So., New York, NY 10016. Copyright 1997 by Foreign Policy Association, Inc. Design by K.M. Rohan. Printed at Science Press, Ephrata, Pennsylvania. Spring 1996. Published October 1997.

Library of Congress Catalog Card No. 97-61135
ISBN 0-87124-178-1

1

The U.S. Role
in the
Post-Cold-War World

EIGHT YEARS HAVE PASSED since the Berlin Wall crumbled, marking the beginning of the end of the cold war, the rollback of Communist domination of Eastern and Central Europe, the dismemberment of the Soviet-led Warsaw Pact military alliance and, ultimately, the collapse of the Soviet Union itself. The destruction of the wall separating the Communist East from the democratic West also closed an era. For 40 years, containing the Soviet threat had been the primary focus of U.S. foreign policy and shaped America's role in the world. Francis Fukuyama, in a widely quoted book, wrote that these events could be seen as "the end of history."

If these events truly had signaled the end of history, perhaps there would be little need for the United States to make a conscious determination concerning its role in the new global order. But in fact, history has not ended and the world remains a dangerous place, even if threats to U.S. interests are less ominous than they were during the era of bipolar nuclear confron-

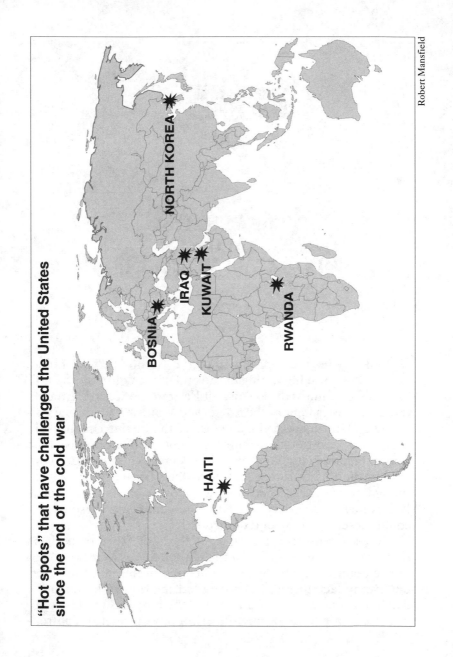

"Hot spots" that have challenged the United States since the end of the cold war

NORTH KOREA

BOSNIA

IRAQ

KUWAIT

RWANDA

HAITI

Robert Mansfield

tation. The dangers include nuclear proliferation and the spread of other weapons of mass destruction, the insidious threat of terrorist attacks, and "small" wars that, at a minimum, inflict suffering on hundreds or thousands of innocent people and, in the extreme, could ignite regional conflicts. Over the longer term, the plight of peoples in the so-called Third World raises the potential for conflicts between "have" and "have-not" populations and nations.

Can the United States, with its overwhelming military superiority, impressive resource base and relative geographic isolation, inoculate itself against these threats? Probably not, as much as it might wish that it could. The world is truly an interdependent place in which U.S. political, economic and security interests can be affected by developments in any region of the globe. Even when U.S. interests are not directly challenged, U.S. values can be called into question by America's actions or, just as likely, its inactions.

Why and how should the United States engage in this much more complex international system, with no wars to fight, no enemy to defend against or defeat? The difficulty of this question is illustrated by the fact that, for several years now, no one answer has resonated with policymakers, experts or the public.

This study raises questions that may help frame the search for a new definition of the U.S. role in the world. It surveys some of the challenges faced by the United States during the past seven years that have begun to shape the U.S. approach to its role in the post-cold-war world and assesses the character and implications of U.S. behavior. With the understanding that consensus may be elusive, it examines some contending perspectives and sets down some possible options for how to proceed on the foreign policy "bridge" to the twenty-first century.

Five Questions

The search for a definition must address five fundamental questions. The questions are simple; the answers, much more difficult. Political leaders probably will not be able to find an organizing principle for the U.S. role in today's world that is as neat and compelling as the cold-war policy of "containment" (i.e., preventing the spread of communism with the aid of free-world alliances). Perhaps the United States will find that it must be content with muddling through for several more years. But if there is a chance of finding a new consensual basis for U.S. foreign policy, the nation, guided by the President and congressional leaders, will have to start addressing these issues now.

➤ *Question No. 1: What do Americans need? In other words, what are vital U.S. interests?* This question has one necessary, but perhaps insufficient, response. The United States needs to be able to protect itself against threats to its territorial integrity and physical security. This task was made much easier by the ending of the cold war and the demise of the Soviet Union. But there is no national consensus on whether or not the United States has other needs or vital interests beyond self-defense.

➤ *Question No. 2: What do Americans want? What are "important" U.S. interests?* One of the key areas for debate is where does the answer to the first question end and the answer to this question begin? The United States clearly would "like" a number of things: a relatively stable international system; good working relations with its friends and allies; continued expansion of the area of democratic governments and free-market economies; answers to humanitarian and ecological problems; and methods of dealing with weapons proliferation and terrorism. Should any of these or other goals be elevated to the area of vital interests, and which ones should remain on the wish list?

➤ *Question No. 3: What do Americans stand for?* Throughout the cold war, U.S. opposition to communism and the expansion of Soviet power was a compelling force for consensus in this country. Americans have already discovered that they coalesced much more effectively out of fear of these threats than they do now out of hope for a better world. The Clinton Administration's decision to hinge its foreign policy on the goal of "enlarging" the area of democracy was greeted by a loud public yawn. But a U.S. foreign policy that is not solidly grounded in American values is hard to imagine. The nation

6

needs to reexamine how its foreign policy relates to its overall system of values and decide which of its goals and commitments remain valid and important in terms of the principles it holds dear.

➤ *Question No. 4: What are Americans willing to pay?* The questions get tougher as they go along. Since the end of the four-decade-long cold war, the United States has been reluctant to "pay" for anything that did not have an obvious and immediate reward. This has been called "instant gratification foreign policy." The Clinton Administration even decided to make "domestic economic well-being" a "pillar" of its national security strategy. Congress has hesitated to vote for funds for military operations and foreign assistance that do not respond to some imminent threat or promise some short-term gain. After the United States had fought for oil-rich Kuwait following the 1990 Iraqi invasion but initially refused to intervene in the civil war in Bosnia, some observers asked critically whether the price of oil had become more important than the political values that inspired U.S. foreign policy.

➤ *Question No. 5: When are Americans willing to risk American lives?* The most difficult decisions for the President and Congress are those that could result in the loss of American lives. Citizens are prepared to make the ultimate sacrifice to defend the United States against direct attack. But are they willing to put troops in harm's way to help police the international system when there is no impending threat to U.S. security? So far, this country has been very reluctant to do so. The danger is, of course, that the longer-term costs of growing international chaos will have to be paid by future generations—and at a higher price.

For now, the Administration, Congress and the public may be able to skate over these slippery issues. But sooner or later they will have to face these five defining questions squarely, even if they cannot always answer them clearly. Allies and potential adversaries alike should know what the United States intends to do with its position as the world's only surviving superpower. Otherwise, they may miscalculate U.S. intentions, with undesirable consequences for all. The challenge of shaping a new world order—and the role of the United States in that order—may mean that the time to raise these questions is now.

2

The International System Today

TODAY, AS THE United States approaches the twenty-first century, there is no commonly accepted characterization of the new international system other than the fact that it has moved beyond the cold war. Nor is there a sense of what kind of world is emerging. The United States and other nations are struggling to shape the system in ways that will support their interests. But the end result is far from clear. This is a transitional period. What are its principal characteristics, at least from the U.S. perspective?

Good News

First, the good news. The international system is relatively congenial to U.S. interests. America is not engaged in a confrontational relationship with any major country or group of countries. The director of the Defense Intelligence Agency, Lt. Gen. Patrick M. Hughes, told Congress in February 1997 that "for at least the next decade, the threats facing the United States will be of a decreased order of magnitude and we will not likely see a global 'peer competitor' within 20 years." The East-West conflict has been replaced by a much more complex picture, one that is filled with a growing number of nations—many with post-Communist societies—attempting to establish a form of democratic governance and a market economy. As a consequence, there is no immediate threat to U.S. survival or even any major challenge to the "American system." Strategically, the United States has some breathing space.

Economically, the United States will always have issues to settle with its trading partners regarding rules as well as the distribution of rewards. The Western economic system thrives on competition tempered by cooperation, because excessive conflict works to everyone's disadvantage. Overall, the current international trading system is one that presents huge opportunities to U.S. businesses and entrepreneurs. A strong domestic economy, the relatively pacific international climate and growing and emerging markets abroad create a generally positive outlook for U.S. interests.

Moreover, the United States has a wide array of friends and potential allies. Now joined against "uncertainty" and "instability," U.S. alliances are changing, but they remain a solid national asset. The most important alliance, the North Atlantic Treaty Organization (NATO) established in 1949 by the United States, Canada and 10 European nations, is being adapted and enlarged to apply the principles of the North Atlantic Treaty to the new security needs of the United States and its allies. U.S. bilateral alliances with key nations in Asia and the Middle East are being updated to reflect current concerns. From this perspective, the globe has never been so favorably inclined toward U.S. interests. This gives the second Clinton Administration and Congress a strong foundation on which to shape a new U.S. role in the world.

Bad News

Now for the bad news. Relations with Russia and China today are poised precariously between elements of cooperation and conflict. Either relationship could go sour in the future.

Either eventuality could destabilize the international system. Russia's reform process is threatened by strong nationalist and former Communist elements, and the direction of its political evolution is largely beyond U.S. influence or control. China is becoming a major player in the international economic system. However, its large and growing market stands in stark contrast to its relatively closed political system, which denies citizens human rights that are taken for granted in Western democracies. China, therefore, remains a potentially disruptive factor in international politics. In addition, North Korea presents a continuing threat to peace on the Korean peninsula and to U.S. forces stationed there to help defend South Korea.

Robert Mansfield

The Middle East is a bubbling cauldron. Israel's survival and security have not yet been ensured by the Middle East peace process. Radical regimes in Libya, Iraq and Iran could endanger regional stability. All three have been, and presumably continue to be, sources of support for international terrorists who, with access to modern weapon technologies, have a widening range of means for attacking civilian targets.

Threats of terrorism and motivations to acquire nuclear, chemical and biological weapons grow out of dissatisfaction with the status quo. A variety of nonproliferation regimes, including the 1968 Treaty on the Non-Proliferation of Nuclear Weapons, exist and the dangers of the spread of these weapons are well-understood in the international community. But weapons of mass destruction remain potentially powerful tools for those who hope to gain advantage over their adversaries. The poor condition of Russian military forces and potential political instability in Russia raise concerns that Russian nuclear weapons might fall into the hands of radical regimes or terrorists. Chinese desires to profit from the international arms market may conflict with U.S. nonproliferation interests. Instability in Russia or China as well as threats to the peace in the Middle East therefore raise profound challenges for the future.

In addition, conditions of poverty, famine and internecine conflict in many regions of the world remain time bombs in an otherwise stable globe. Until underlying economic, social and political problems are resolved or ameliorated, these conditions in Africa, Asia and elsewhere will continue to challenge U.S. values and, potentially, U.S. interests.

Even though the global economic system is largely friendly to the United States, America must ensure that inevitable conflicts that arise are resolved before they harm U.S. interests or disrupt U.S. political and security relationships with trading partners.

Challenges Confronting the United States

According to the U.S. intelligence community, the main problems facing the United States include:

● the continuing transformation of Russia and the evolution of China;

● those states—North Korea, Iran, Iraq—whose hostile policies toward the United States and its allies could undermine regional stability;

● transnational issues, including terrorism, proliferation of weapons of mass destruction, international drug trafficking, growth in international organized crime and threats to U.S. information systems;

● regional "hot spots" that could explode, such as the Middle East, the South Asian subcontinent and Bosnia;

● countries and regions crippled by human misery; nations involved in, or unable to cope with, ethnic and civil conflict, forced migration, refugee flows and the possibility of large-scale deaths—all potentially placing demands on U.S. military and intelligence capabilities.

The current international system, therefore, presents the United States with a variety of challenges as well as immense opportunities. As President Bill Clinton stated in his February 1997 State of the Union address, "With the cold war receding and global commerce at record levels, we are helping to win an unrivaled peace and prosperity all across the world.... But now we must rise to the decisive moment to make a nation and a world better than any we have ever known."

While the United States has been searching for a new definition of its role in the emerging international system, the country has been compelled to act and, in particular, to weigh its use of force. A close examination of those challenges and responses may help Americans recognize and understand the road they have traveled since the end of the cold war, before they consider where they may go from here.

3

Challenges and Responses

SINCE THE END of the cold war, the world has experienced a wide range of localized wars, aggressions and violations of internationally accepted human rights and humanitarian standards. The United States has had to shape diplomatic responses and design policies to mitigate future challenges to U.S. interests by promoting peace negotiations in the Middle East and Bosnia and engaging in arms-control discussions. In a number of circumstances, the United States and its allies have used force to confront aggressors or to facilitate the settlement of disputes.

The response of the international community—no longer strictly polarized by cold-war divisions and theoretically more free to organize collectively in reaction to specific security challenges—has been uneven and hard to predict. One of the most important reasons for this mixed record has been the world community's continued reliance on U.S. leadership and military forces at a time when the United States has been questioning its own obligations and willingness to play such a role. This dependence reveals habits of deference developed during the cold war, particularly among Western allies of the United States. It also underscores the U.S. position as the sole-surviving superpower.

As the post-cold-war international world began to emerge, no other country matched America's potential for leadership. No country had the military power or a global outreach equal to that of the United States. No other country (or group of countries, including the 15-nation European Union or the United Nations collectively) appeared to have the potential to take America's place, particularly when it came to projecting political leadership and military force beyond national borders.

Nothing has done more to test the U.S. concept of its role in the world than challenges in which the use of force is an option. Since the end of the cold war, a number of international crises and conflicts have raised this issue. The U.S. responses help illustrate some trends in the U.S. approach to its leadership role.

The Persian Gulf War and a 'New World Order'

In August 1990, the invasion of Kuwait by the forces of Iraqi leader Saddam Hussein provided the first post-cold-war test of the ability of the international community to respond to a clear case of aggression. Following U.S. leadership and relying heavily on U.S. forces, the international community acted with a UN mandate. It reversed Iraq's aggression, restored Kuwaiti independence and imposed sanctions on a defeated Iraq. The latter were designed both to punish the Iraqis and to make any future act of aggression there or elsewhere more dangerous and more costly.

Many observers saw the international community's cooperation in responding to the Iraqi invasion as a hopeful sign for the post-cold-war world. The experience suggested that the UN Security Council might finally be able to operate effectively as a peacekeeper. The UN Charter adopted in 1945 had granted the Security Council primary responsibility for maintaining the peace, but the cold war between the superpowers had limited its ability to carry out that role. Most people hoped that nonmilitary means, such as preventive diplomacy, economic assistance and the threat or use of economic sanctions, would be the instruments of first resort to discourage aggression and other violations of internationally accepted norms of behavior. But very few believed that the world would be peaceful unless the international community spoke softly *and* carried a big stick.

To help justify and build support for the military response to the Iraqi aggression, President George Bush (1989–93) stated that his actions were part of an emerging "new world order" in which the United States would play a leading role. This new order, according to Bush, would feature increased U.S.-Soviet cooperation, a more effective UN and multilateral responses to threats to this order.

But once the American-led Desert Storm operations had driven Iraqi forces out of Kuwait in February 1991, Bush seemed to retreat from his new-world-order policy. His approach was questioned by critics who represented a wide variety of perspectives. Many criticized it for relying too heavily on the use of military force, a strong U.S. leadership role and the involvement of international organizations. As the Administration turned its attention to domestic priorities and the forthcoming presidential election campaign, the new-world-order concept became the first foreign policy orphan of the post-cold-war era.

Bush's subsequent retreat from his attempt to establish a wider framework for a U.S. role could be viewed as the product of the first serious questioning of whether the United States had the obligation or the ability to continue to lead as it had during the cold war.

Somalia: Retreat from Responsibility?

The U.S. intervention in Somalia raised serious doubts about future U.S. willingness to use force on behalf of foreign policy objectives. On November 25, 1992, following defeat in his bid for reelection, Bush made one more international commitment on behalf of the United States when he offered to participate in a multinational force to help create basic security in Somalia.

That country on the Horn of East Africa was suffering nearly anarchic internal strife resulting in widespread famine, and relief supplies were not reaching needy Somalis.

According to the Bush plan, the U.S.-led force would create safe conditions to permit relief supplies to reach the starving and it would then transfer its security function to UN peacekeepers. The UN approved a U.S.-led military force to guarantee distribution of food (UN Security Council Resolution 794) on December 3, 1992. The President observed that "the United States alone cannot right the world's wrongs, but we know that some crises in the world cannot be resolved without American involvement....Only the United States has the global reach to place a large security force on the ground in such a distant place quickly and efficiently and, thus, save thousands of innocents from death." Ironically, subsequent events in Somalia would undermine U.S. willingness to play the role envisioned in the Bush statement.

U.S. troops began landing in Somalia on December 9, taking over responsibility for the security of relief operations from the small UN force of 500 Pakistani soldiers who had arrived in October. This expeditionary force helped create peaceful enough conditions to allow relief efforts to deal with the famine. U.S. forces suffered their first casualty on January 12, 1993—eight days before Clinton's inauguration. The new Administration supported continuation of the effort, and both the Senate and the House approved the use of force on behalf of the UN mission in the spring of 1993.

In June 1993, forces loyal to one of the Somali warlords,

Gen. Mohamed Farah Aidid, ambushed Pakistani peacekeepers, killing 23. The UN, in response, authorized the arrest of Aidid, and one week later a bounty was put out for him. By the summer of 1993, some members of Congress were growing concerned about "mission creep"—the expansion of the U.S. role which had begun with the United States protecting relief efforts and ended with U.S. forces joining in the Somali civil war against Aidid.

On September 25, three U.S. soldiers were killed when their helicopter was shot down, further increasing domestic anxiety about the costs of U.S. involvement. Public concern rose dramatically when, on October 3, 18 U.S. soldiers were killed in an attempt to capture Aidid's top lieutenants. U.S. television broadcast pictures of U.S. casualties, including the body of one U.S. soldier being dragged through the streets of Mogadishu, Somalia's capital, by Aidid's supporters.

In reaction, some members of Congress called for the immediate withdrawal of U.S. forces from Somalia. Critics of the Administration charged that the United States had allowed itself to be dragged into a "nation-building" exercise that was much different from the original, limited humanitarian relief effort. Others complained that U.S. forces in Somalia had become instruments of a UN mission, within a command structure and combat organization that placed U.S. forces in jeopardy. According to this view, the UN was not capable of mounting military operations in dangerous circumstances, and U.S. soldiers had been required to rely on less-competent military units from other countries.

Clinton responded by sending additional U.S. forces to Somalia to prevent further casualties and promised to withdraw all U.S. forces by March 31, 1994. On October 15, 1993, the Senate approved an amendment to the fiscal year (FY) 1994 defense appropriations bill endorsing Clinton's plan for a March 1994 pullout. The senators had previously rejected an amendment calling for a "prompt" withdrawal. On January 28, 1994, the UN undersecretary general in charge of peacekeeping (and now UN secretary-general), Kofi Annan, observed that "the impression has been created that the easiest way to disrupt a peacekeeping operation is to kill Americans." The U.S. mission officially ended on March 25, 1994.

The U.S. intervention in Somalia appears to have convinced many Americans that the United States should not take serious risks or pay a significant price in blood or money to restore order in parts of the world of little immediate relevance to vital U.S. interests. The American public generally had been sympathetic to the original mission of a U.S. presence in Somalia to create sufficiently stable conditions so that humanitarian assistance could reach the population. When the mission was expanded to include involvement in Somalia's civil conflict, Congress and the public began to question the commitment.

The domestic reaction to the deaths of the U.S. soldiers caused the government to question the objectives, wisdom and importance of the humanitarian mission and the arrangements under which American forces had been deployed. The Clinton Administration had been laboring for almost nine months on a policy regarding international peace operations that called for the United States to place greater reliance on international organizations, particularly the UN. The October 3 massacre of the 18 Americans apparently confirmed the Administration officials' emerging judgment that they would have to produce a much more circumspect set of objectives and guidelines for future U.S. peacekeeping operations.

Bosnia: From Avoidance to Leadership

Within a year of the victory in the Persian Gulf war, the deterrent value of the international response to Iraqi aggression was challenged by the increasingly cautious U.S. policy toward the use of force. As the United States became immersed in its first national election of the post-cold-war era, fighting broke out in former Yugoslavia in June 1991. Bush decided not to lead or even participate actively in attempts to prevent or control the growing conflict. The Administration relied largely on efforts by the members of the European Community (the precursor of the European Union) to negotiate a peaceful settlement. The Bush Administration's hands-off approach regarding Yugoslavia undoubtedly was influenced by the inherent complexity of the Balkan situation, the unlikelihood of an early resolution and the strong opposition from U.S. military officials to any commitment of U.S. forces. The latter, combined with European reticence to act and the approach of the 1992 presidential election campaign, militated against a potentially costly intervention in former Yugoslavia. In retrospect, many observers now believe an early intervention would have been less costly in the long run.

During the campaign, candidate Clinton criticized President Bush for failing to respond to the crisis in former Yugoslavia. After taking office, however, President Clinton retreated from the greater involvement implied by his campaign rhetoric. The new Administration instead adopted a policy of willingness to contribute U.S. peacekeeping forces, but only after the warring parties agreed to a settlement; it would not send forces under other circumstances. The Administration sought the support of its NATO allies to lift the arms embargo imposed by the UN in 1991 in order to provide additional weapons to the Bosnian government's Muslim forces. At the same time, it planned to conduct air strikes against the Bosnian Serbs to achieve a military situation more conducive to a peace settlement. But when the Administration encountered European opposition, it backed down.

Following the failed attempt to promote a "lift and strike" approach, the United States supported enforcement of a "no-fly" zone over former Yugoslavia. It also participated in threats by NATO to carry out air strikes against Bosnian Serb forces attacking the Bosnian capital of Sarajevo and five other "safe areas." U.S. planes actually mounted some limited air strikes on Bosnian Serb forces. Further, the United States contributed ships to the international fleet implementing the economic embargo against Serbia and played an active role in support of relief shipments to Bosnia. In 1994, the United States joined a "contact group" composed of Russia, Britain, France and Germany in seeking to arrange a political settlement. In addition,

Bosnia, Where NATO Forces, Including 8,500 Americans, Keep the Peace

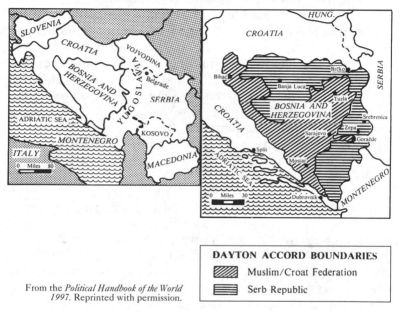

DAYTON ACCORD BOUNDARIES

From the *Political Handbook of the World 1997.* Reprinted with permission.

the Administration sent a small peacekeeping unit to support a Nordic military presence in the breakaway Former Yugoslav Republic of Macedonia.

The Clinton Administration continued to affirm that it wanted to see the UN arms embargo lifted to allow weapon shipments to the Bosnian government's Muslim forces. But, when Congress pressured the Administration to aid in the defense of these forces against the Bosnian Serbs, it refused to act unilaterally. The Administration argued that such an action could harm peace efforts and relations with allied nations.

Until mid-1995, the United States continued to insist that it would commit ground forces to Bosnia only if there were a peace settlement to enforce and a number of other conditions were met. These included NATO (not UN) command of any enforcement operations; clear political and military strategies, including an "exit strategy"; plans for financing the operation; and support from Congress for the commitment.

Even though the Clinton Administration had pursued what could arguably be called an "activist" strategy toward the Bosnian issue, the truth was that no one was eager in mid-1995 to commit the United States in Bosnia under circumstances that could produce heavy casualties among U.S. forces. Even those advancing the most impassioned arguments in the congressional debate over lifting the arms embargo in order to "do something" for the beleaguered Bosnians assumed that it would be politically impossible to commit U.S. ground forces until a peace settlement had been reached.

U.S. Leadership Questioned Abroad

In spite of the UN economic embargo against Serbia, enforcement of a no-fly zone and limited air strikes against Serbian forces, the Bosnian Serb military and political leadership appeared to be undeterred. As long as the international presence in Bosnia was limited to protection of humanitarian relief operations and certain isolated safe areas, the Bosnian Serbs continued to use military force to wrest control of territory from the Bosnian government. The threats of military action against the Serbian forces lacked credibility if the United States and its NATO allies were unwilling to use ground forces to back up such threats. When air strikes were mounted, they were so limited they undermined their credibility as a military threat to the main Serbian forces. It cannot be known whether a more forceful U.S. and international approach would have produced an earlier end to the conflict. But the U.S. unwillingness to put its military forces in harm's way in Bosnia prompted people in Europe and around the world to question the U.S. will or ability to lead the international community in occasions of localized civil strife or even dangerous regional aggression.

In mid-1995, the ground began to shift dramatically. The French and British governments, which provided most of the troops in the UN Protection Force (Unprofor) in Bosnia, considered giving up their mission. As conditions worsened, the United States took the helm and initiated a negotiating process that eventually led to the peace accords that were signed in Dayton, Ohio, on December 17, 1995, and the creation of a NATO-led Implementation Force (IFOR). Most observers also credit Croatian military advances against Serbian-held territory and intensive NATO air strikes for preparing the way for the Dayton agreement. In spite of strong congressional misgivings and without formal congressional support, the United States played the leading role in IFOR, which was authorized by the UN Security Council. It supplied close to one half of the ground forces (over 25,000 of the 60,000) and, arguably, contributed more to the force's credibility than the other countries combined. In December 1996, IFOR "completed" its mission of establishing a peaceful military setting for the process of civilian reconstruction. It was succeeded by a much smaller NATO Stabilization Force (SFOR), in which the United States remains the major player and contributor of forces (some 8,500 out of roughly 35,000). The United States and its allies must decide what to do when the SFOR mandate expires in June 1998.

In the Bosnian case, the United States appears at first to have searched for an approach that would confirm traditional U.S. opposition to aggression, genocide and gross violations of human rights without risking American lives. Because U.S. vital interests were not directly threatened, the Clinton Administration, Congress and the American people initially were reluctant to pay the price of deploying U.S. ground forces to Bosnia. The Administration ultimately intervened to facilitate and then to implement a peace accord. It did so when it appeared to the Administration that U.S. intervention would be the only way to prevent a catastrophe for Bosnia and restore the credibility of NATO and U.S. leadership in Europe.

Haiti: An 'Intermestic' Issue

After much hesitation, the United States ultimately used overwhelming force to restore an elected government in the Caribbean island of Haiti. Haiti is a special case in U.S. foreign policy. Its geographic proximity to the United States and the impact of Haitian refugees on Florida, in particular, make it an important domestic issue as well as an international problem— referred to by some as an intermestic issue. If Haiti were several thousand miles across the ocean, the return of democracy to this small nation would most likely have been a low priority among U.S. foreign policy objectives.

After a military coup overthrew the democratically elected government of President Jean-Bertrand Aristide in September 1991, the Bush Administration sought to encourage the restoration of that government and a return to democracy, largely through imposition of economic sanctions and diplomatic pressure on the coup's leaders. In 1993–94, the Clinton Administration intensified pressure on the military rulers. The White House was motivated by the problems that the influx of Haitian refugees was creating for a key electoral state, Florida; humanitarian concern for the refugees, highlighted by a hunger strike on their behalf by prominent African-American leader Randall Robinson of TransAfrica; a commitment to enlarging the area of democracy in the world; and significant pressure from African-American members of Congress to restore democracy and acceptable human-rights conditions in Haiti.

The implied U.S. threat to use force in Haiti may not have appeared credible to the Haitian junta. In October 1993, shortly after the deaths of 18 Americans in Somalia, the United States dispatched a ship carrying part of a 1,300-member UN contingent that included Americans and Canadians to Haiti. The Haitian military leadership had agreed to allow the troops to land, but an angry mob at the dock (presumably organized by the junta) appeared to threaten a peaceful disembarkation, and the U.S. cargo ship *Harlan County* turned back. U.S. officials subsequently acknowledged that the U.S. experience in Somalia had influenced their decision not to risk casualties by landing the troops. The sequence of events was widely interpreted as a confrontation between unequals in which the United States blinked first. It was a major victory for the junta and a serious setback for the Clinton Administration's credibility.

24

In the months preceding U.S. intervention, it was unclear whether or not Congress favored the commitment of forces to Haiti. Some members who were particularly concerned about gross violations of human rights in Haiti under the dictatorship urged the use of force to overthrow the regime, but others were undecided. On October 21, 1993, the U.S. Senate defeated (by a vote of 81–19) an amendment, offered by Senator Jesse A. Helms (R-N.C.), chairman of the Foreign Relations Committee, that would have blocked deployment of U.S. troops to Haiti without prior congressional authorization except to protect or evacuate U.S. citizens. The Senate did approve (by a vote of 98–2) a "sense of the Congress" amendment, offered by Senator George A. Mitchell (D-Me.), that urged the President to seek congressional authorization before committing U.S. troops to Haiti. On May 24, 1994, the House passed a nonbinding resolution opposing an invasion of Haiti. On June 9, it voted again and reversed its decision.

On June 29, the Senate rejected another Republican-led effort to require the President to seek congressional authorization before ordering military intervention in Haiti. In lieu of such authorization, the President could have submitted a written report to Congress on the objectives of such a mission. This amendment was defeated by a vote of 65–34. The Senate then voted 93–4 to approve a nonbinding amendment urging the President to seek congressional approval before sending troops to Haiti. These votes suggest that most senators were reluctant to tie the President's hands in his role as commander in chief. In spite of various reservations concerning Administration policy toward Haiti, they preferred that the President bear responsibility for any decision to use force to remove the junta.

Use of Overwhelming U.S. Force Attains Objective

On September 19, 1994, the United States began deploying some 16,000 military forces to Haiti. Just prior to their arrival, during the visit of a U.S. delegation that included former President Jimmy Carter (1977–81), the Haitian military rulers had agreed to relinquish power. They had signed an agreement allowing the immediate, unopposed entry of U.S. troops and the return to power of President Aristide. The large U.S. force met no organized resistance. On March 31, 1995, in accordance with the Administration's plan, the U.S.-led mission gave way to a UN peacekeeping operation. By mid-April 1996, all but 200 U.S. military engineers had been removed from Haiti.

The overall impression left by Administration and congressional handling of the Haitian situation was that the United States would have much preferred not to use force to oust the military junta and restore the democratic government to power. The pressure to do so resulted largely from the humanitarian and financial problems created by the exodus of Haitians from the island.

As it happened, the deployment to Haiti met the primary objective of restoring civilian rule without serious loss of Haitian lives and with only one U.S. combat casualty. The use of overwhelming force in this case apparently served to deter any attempt by the Haitian junta or its supporters to retain power. The absence of serious casualties helped mitigate congressional and public opposition to the operation.

North Korea: A Persistent Problem

In 1993–94, the question of the use of force in North Korea to support U.S. nonproliferation goals and to honor the long-standing commitment to defend South Korea against possible aggression from North Korea confronted U.S. policymakers. The crisis was touched off by North Korea's decision in March 1993 to suspend international inspections of its nuclear facilities and to withdraw from the Treaty on the Non-Proliferation of Nuclear Weapons, which it had signed in 1985. The actions came after the International Atomic Energy Agency (IAEA) found evidence that North Korea had produced more weapons-grade plutonium than it had admitted, which suggested an intent to divert the material for nuclear-weapons production.

During the maneuvering between the United States and North Korea after March 1993, the Clinton Administration vacillated between a hard-line position and a more conciliatory approach. For example, in March 1994, Secretary of Defense William J. Perry said that the United States intended, even at the risk of war, to stop North Korea from developing a substantial arsenal of nuclear weapons. Then, in June 1994, the Administration, apparently at the urging of Jimmy Carter, gave the former President tacit sanction to undertake a mediating mission to North Korea. After meeting with North Korea's leader, Kim Il Sung, on June 15 and 16, Carter announced that Kim intended to pursue "good faith efforts" to resolve the crisis and the United States could therefore relax its stance. (Kim died three weeks later.) The visit stimulated planning for a North-South Korean summit and, at least temporarily, moved the Administration away from its earlier hard-line position.

Most experts agree that war on the Korean peninsula would be devastating for all concerned. Although the United States and South Korea would presumably defeat a North Korean attack, the conflict could result in the destruction of Seoul, South Korea's capital and economic and population center. It could also mean many casualties for U.S. and South Korean forces. Thirty-seven thousand U.S. troops stand astride the likely invasion routes.

U.S. counterproliferation strikes against North Korean nuclear facilities presumably would be viewed by the North as an act of war, possibly setting off a larger war. Alternatively, a U.S. threat to use force in the absence of an unprovoked North Korean attack on South Korea probably would look like a bluff to North Korea.

PDD-25's Constraints on Intervention

When Presidential Decision Directive 25 (PDD-25) was issued in May 1994, it reflected the Administration's recent experiences in Somalia, Bosnia and Haiti, as well as congressional debates of the previous year. Consequently, the directive represented a substantial modification of the Clinton Administration's original concept of U.S. participation in UN peace operations, and it incorporated many of the limitations on U.S. commitments suggested by congressional responses to the casualties in Somalia. In June 1993, the Administration rejected the policy of "assertive multilateralism" espoused by U.S. Ambassador to the UN Madeleine K. Albright. Instead, it adopted PDD-25's policy of "stringent conditionality."

PDD-25 laid out a long list of factors that the United States would consider when voting on peace operations in the UN Security Council. These conditions included the following: whether UN involvement advances U.S. interests; if a threat to the peace exists; whether there are clear objectives and the means to accomplish the mission; whether the consequences of inaction have been weighed and are considered to be unacceptable; and whether the operation's duration is tied to clear objectives and realistic criteria for ending it (an exit strategy).

PDD-25 detailed even more demanding additional factors to be weighed for operations involving U.S. participation. Those factors, many of which were prominently mentioned in the October 1993 congressional debate on U.S. participation in peace operations, included whether or not

- risks to American personnel are considered acceptable;
- personnel, funds and other resources are available;
- U.S. participation is necessary for the success of any operation;
- the role of U.S. forces is tied to clear objectives and an end point for U.S. participation can be identified;
- domestic and congressional support exists or can be marshaled; and
- command and control arrangements are acceptable.

If it is anticipated that U.S. involvement will include combat, PDD-25 goes on to list factors that reflect the U.S. military establishment's legitimate concerns. These factors, which appear to be drawn directly from the military's institutional reaction to the Vietnam War, include whether or not there is

- a determination to commit sufficient forces to achieve clearly defined objectives;
- a plan to achieve those objectives decisively; and
- a commitment to reassess and adjust the size, composition and disposition of forces to achieve U.S. objectives.

It is possible to look at these extensive lists of prior considerations and reach a variety of conclusions. Most of the conditions, taken individually, appear reasonable under most circumstances. Taken collectively, however, against the backdrop of
experiences with the use of force in the post-cold-war world,
they appear so constraining as to inhibit any action.

Rwanda: A Test for the New Peacekeeping Policy

The civil war in Rwanda presented the first opportunity to
apply the Clinton Administration's PDD-25 approach to peace
operations. This crisis was precipitated when Rwanda's president, Juvénal Habyarimana, and the president of Burundi died
in a plane crash near Kigali, Rwanda's capital, on April 6, 1994.
The plane was rumored to have been hit by rocket fire, but the
cause of the crash has never been determined. Some sources
claimed that the forces of the Tutsi ethnic minority were responsible. (Habyarimana was a Hutu, Rwanda's ethnic majority.) On the other hand, other reports suggested that Hutus carried out the attack to undermine a plan for settlement of the
Tutsi-Hutu ethnic conflict that they regarded as unfavorable.

The fighting immediately following the crash took the lives
of 200,000 to 500,000 Rwandans. Most were Tutsi who were
slaughtered by Hutus, led by the presidential guard and the
militia. An estimated 1.5 million were rendered homeless in
Rwanda, and similar numbers fled to neighboring Zaire and
Uganda. Subsequently, Tutsi rebel forces, trained outside
Rwanda, reversed the Hutu gains and ultimately seized the
entire country.

Prior to this conflict, the UN had sent a 2,500-member UN
Assistance Mission for Rwanda (Unamir) to help implement a
Hutu-Tutsi peace accord reached in August 1993. The force,
under a Canadian commander, consisted of some 940 soldiers
from Ghana, 840 from Bangladesh and 440 from Belgium. After
losing 10 soldiers in the fighting, Belgium withdrew its contingent, and the UN Security Council on April 22, 1994, decided
to reduce the remaining force to 270 military and civilian personnel. In June, France sent more than 2,500 troops to Rwanda

with the Security Council's endorsement. The French government described this move as a temporary humanitarian operation to protect innocent civilians until the international community acted to produce a longer-term solution.

From the outset of the crisis, it was clear that the United States would not volunteer to send troops to Rwanda. In addition, the United States raised questions about sending any new troops to reinforce Unamir and urged a go-slow approach. It blocked, or at least delayed, UN Security Council Resolution 918 of May 1994 to authorize a 5,500-person force for Rwanda, arguing that more time was needed to plan such a force. The United States did offer to lease 50 M-113 armored personnel carriers (APCs) to the UN for use in Rwanda. But the Administration remained consistent with PDD-25's cautionary approach to U.S. contributions to UN peacekeeping and mindful of congressional sentiments in favor of keeping U.S. peacekeeping costs limited. To this end, the Administration engaged in protracted negotiations over how much the UN would pay the United States for the use of the APCs.

Another indication of the Administration's circumspect approach was its position on whether or not genocide existed in Rwanda. The 1948 Genocide Convention, to which the United States is a party, implies that nations have an obligation to respond in cases of genocide. The Administration on June 9, 1994, instructed its spokesperson to say only that "acts of genocide may have occurred," apparently seeking to diminish or defer U.S. responsibility to act. The Administration, faced with protests by members of Congress and human-rights groups, eventually condemned the killings as genocide but never made any change in its approach to the crisis.

Critics have charged that the U.S. government contributed to the deaths of thousands of Rwandan civilians. Supporters of the Clinton Administration reject the charge. They argue that the United States had no economic or security interests at stake in Rwanda, only humanitarian concerns, and therefore should not have become militarily involved. Between July and September 1994, the United States did mount "Operation Support

"WHICH ONES ARE THE POOR STARVING REFUGEES AND WHICH ONES ARE THE BLOODCURDLING GENOCIDAL MANIACS?"

Hope," in which nearly 2,600 U.S. troops assisted with logistics for relief supplies and provided help to refugee camps in Zaire.

In November 1996, the United States was pressed by several of its allies to join in a humanitarian relief effort in Zaire. The United States remained reluctant to provide the necessary airlift for the operation, and the intended multinational refugee-rescue effort was never mounted. The Clinton Administration's caution was induced partly by the fact that, as the refugee camps in eastern Zaire were broken up in late 1996, hundreds of thousands of refugees began returning to Rwanda.

The Zaire crisis came to a head in 1997 as rebel forces led by Laurent Kabila overthrew long-time Zaire President Mobutu Sese Seko, who fled the country. Kabila renamed Zaire the Democratic Republic of the Congo. U.S. Ambassador to the UN Bill Richardson visited the region just prior to the rebel victory to help ensure a relatively peaceful transition. Whether or not the Kabila regime will promote stability and democracy in the troubled country remains to be seen.

Should the United States have taken a more interventionist

approach to the Rwandan crisis is a question that will be debated. But the Clinton Administration's response tended to support the perception that the United States was increasingly reluctant to use military force in circumstances where U.S. interests were not threatened.

Limiting Resources for Foreign Policy

During this period of American reticence regarding foreign intervention, the United States has also been reducing the resources available for implementing its foreign policy. Spending on international affairs agencies, which began falling in the mid-1980s, has dropped some 50 percent since 1984. There are several explanations for this decline. Funding for foreign aid and for the main foreign policy agencies (principally the Department of State), which have virtually no domestic constituencies, has always been vulnerable. Given the receding threats to U.S. interests since the end of the cold war, the desire to reduce U.S. global involvement and pressures to trim the U.S. federal budget deficit, large cuts were almost inevitable. In explaining these pressures, it should be noted that most Americans have a distorted view of just how much the United States spends on its foreign policy. Polls suggest that a majority of Americans believe that 15 percent or more of the U.S. budget is spent on foreign aid alone. In fact, foreign aid amounts to only some seven tenths of one percent. The FY 1997 budget of $18.3 billion for all foreign policy agencies and programs, including foreign aid, is but one percent of total federal budget authority. Both Administration projections and congressional plans suggest further cuts.

Outgoing Secretary of State Warren M. Christopher (1993–96) warned that continued decline in the U.S. international affairs budget would undermine the ability of the United States to defend its interests around the world. It would also compel the United States to resort to the use of force more often. Speaking to West Point cadets on October 25, 1996, Christopher argued that the United States needed sufficient resources to pursue effective relations with major powers, to play a key role in international organizations, to support U.S. business interests overseas, and to maintain adequate representational and communications facilities around the world. Christopher's successor, Madeleine Albright, has echoed his concerns. Other factors complicate the picture. Well before the end of the cold war, many experts felt that the U.S. foreign assistance program needed reform. There is general support for foreign aid that goes toward supporting the Middle East peace process, for humanitarian relief efforts and for narcotics-control activities. But there is no such consensus on aid to other parts of the world, or for other purposes. There are, furthermore, fundamental disagreements about the extent to which foreign aid can effectively produce economic development.

Division Over U.S. Debt to UN

In recent years, calls for reform of the UN also have caused a deep split between the Administration and Congress. There has been agreement that reform is needed, and this belief was a major factor influencing the successful U.S. campaign to replace Boutros Boutros-Ghali as UN secretary-general. Influential members of Congress have argued that the United States should make payment of back dues to the UN dependent on reform. The Clinton Administration wants to repay the debt in order to prevent further deterioration in U.S. influence on decisionmaking in the organization.

In 1997, Administration and congressional positions converged somewhat, leading to legislation that would pay U.S. arrears to UN budgets over the next several years. This would only happen if the Administration could certify that the UN system was being reformed. In spite of this progress, resolution of the issue may depend on working out some difficult details, including the discrepancy between the UN estimate of the U.S. debt and the total accepted by the Administration and Congress, which is substantially lower.

The last few years have also seen a legislative-executive debate on reorganizing U.S. foreign policy agencies. Several members of Congress proposed merging three smaller foreign

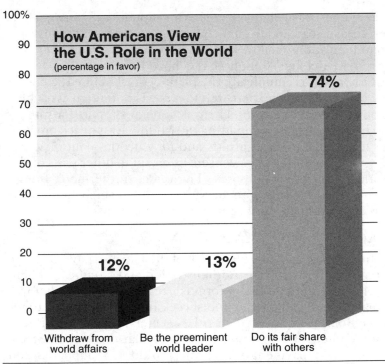

How Americans View the U.S. Role in the World
(percentage in favor)

Withdraw from world affairs	Be the preeminent world leader	Do its fair share with others
12%	13%	74%

Source: Center for International and Security Studies at the University of Maryland and its Program on International Policy Attitudes (PIPA), July 10, 1996.

policy organizations—the U.S. Agency for International Development (AID), the U.S. Information Agency (USIA) and the U.S. Arms Control and Disarmament Agency (ACDA)—into the U.S. Department of State. Some Administration officials agreed that consolidation could be useful. Others argued that each of these smaller agencies exists because, without its autonomy, its area of responsibility would not receive appropriate priority. Merger with the State Department would diminish the effectiveness, respectively, of foreign aid programs, public diplomacy and arms-control policy. Nevertheless, the Administration has now initiated a process of consolidation.

These issues have been difficult to resolve in the absence of a broader agreement on the goals that the United States should pursue in the world. According to public opinion polls, the American people, by substantial majorities, still want the United States to play a world leadership role. But they do not want the United States to be the world's policeman; they want it to share the leadership function with others. This may be the beginning of an emerging consensus.

4

Factors That Influence U.S. Foreign Policy

T HE FOREGOING REVIEW of events suggests that America's post-cold-war reluctance to play a decisive international role arises from a combination of circumstances and independent policy choices. The circumstances include the changes in the international environment at the end of the cold war. The choices are those that have been made by the Bush and Clinton Administrations and also by the U.S. Congress. From the survey of some of the challenges of the past several years, it appears that the United States has been experiencing an "escapist" period in its history. What has contributed to that escapism?

No Threats to Vital U.S. Interests

The most important circumstantial influence on U.S. attitudes is that, once the cold war had ended, the Warsaw Pact (the Soviet-East European military alliance formed in response to NATO) had closed shop and the Soviet Union had dissolved, the United States faced few real and present dangers to its national security.

During the cold war, U.S. Presidents were able to argue convincingly that the vital U.S. interest of national survival in a free community of nations was threatened by the purposeful spread of Communist ideology and the power of the Soviet Union and China, the major Communist states. Only one aspect of this challenge, the Soviet Union's strategic nuclear forces, posed an imminent threat to national survival. Other threats and sources of instability were seen as extensions of the main threat. In response, the United States fought wars in Korea (1950-53) and Vietnam (1960-75), deployed large military forces armed with nuclear weapons in Europe, and intervened in or supported military actions in Middle Eastern, African and Latin American countries, all in support of a global defense against the Communist threat.

Today, aggressions and sources of instability that in the cold war might have been seen as extensions of the Soviet threat warranting a U.S. military response appear much less dangerous to vital U.S. interests. This has left the United States without a sense of foreign policy purpose to replace that of containing Communist expansion and Soviet power.

Cold-War-Leadership Fatigue

With the notable exception of President Bush, who continued to savor foreign policy involvement to the very end of his term, many Americans in the early 1990s appeared to be experiencing what might be called cold-war-leadership fatigue. The perception of the American people was that the United States had carried the lion's share of defense responsibilities and burdens throughout the cold war. Although public opinion recognized that the United States could not adopt an isolationist posture, most Americans apparently wished to escape the extensive global tasks that the United States had performed for over four decades as the center of a worldwide alliance.

The popular preference for attention to domestic issues, suggested by the 1992 election, did not necessarily indicate that the public wanted the United States to retreat from an international leadership role. After the negative experience in Somalia, one poll in the spring of 1994 found the public wary of "repeating Somalia mistakes" in Bosnia and of getting bogged down in "another Vietnam." The same poll nonetheless discovered that "strong majorities found convincing the arguments that the United States should intervene to stop the bloodshed [in Bosnia] for moral reasons, that it would show poor leadership for the United States not to contribute troops when it has been a major proponent of a peace agreement, and that ethnic cleansing is a form of genocide that must be stopped." More recent polls have revealed similar attitudes toward U.S. leadership in general, and U.S. involvement in Bosnia in particular.

It is by no means clear, however, that popular majorities could be sustained if the U.S. presence in Bosnia or elsewhere were to produce U.S. casualties or require the transfer of significant funds from domestic programs and deficit reduction to military spending.

Limited Tolerance for Casualties

Whether or not the United States is willing to risk the lives of its young soldiers for international causes is an emotional question and a critical judgmental factor that affects the ability of the United States to use force on behalf of its foreign policy objectives. Examination of this issue reveals a variety of perspectives.

One analyst has argued that a major reason the United States and other postindustrial societies are reluctant to use force in their foreign relations is their reduced tolerance for casualties of war. According to political-military analyst Edward N. Luttwak, large families and high infant mortality were the norm in former great powers throughout history. Under those circumstances, according to Luttwak, "To lose a young family member for any reason was always tragic no doubt, yet his death in combat was not the extraordinary and fundamentally unacceptable event that it has now become."

According to this analysis, only "exceptionally determined leaders" are capable of overcoming the societal resistance to casualties in postindustrial societies. Luttwak cites President Bush in the Persian Gulf conflict and British Prime Minister Margaret Thatcher in the Falkland Islands episode. (In response to Argentina's invasion of the disputed islands in the South Atlantic in April 1982, Britain dispatched an armada and regained control.) Without effective leadership, resistance to casualties is so high that postindustrial societies generally elect to use their military forces only for the defense of narrowly defined vital interests or when casualties are gauged to be minimal.

Harry Summers, a former military officer who writes on defense matters, takes issue with what he views as Luttwak's "admiration" for the imperialist great powers. According to Summers, "The value of military intervention in Bosnia, Somalia, Haiti and North Korea has not been established. Therefore, at face value, the cost in terms of casualties is prohibitive."

It is not necessary to accept Luttwak's historical analysis to conclude that current tolerance in the United States for military casualties is low. Whether or not the U.S. public or other Western electorates would be willing to accept heavy casualties in a case where important national interests were more directly threatened is not clear. There has not been such a case in recent history, and there may not be one for some time to come. (Korea and Vietnam each cost over 50,000 U.S. lives, and in both cases public support dwindled when victory was not achieved.) Whatever the circumstances, it is clear that the American people remain reluctant to accept casualties without a sense of significant purpose or mission for which their soldiers are asked to risk their lives.

Cautious U.S. Military Leadership

The "bad" and "good" experiences of U.S. armed forces in recent decades have made a strong impact on professional military leaders. The number one "bad" experience—the war in Vietnam—reinforced their conviction that they should not undertake missions that could not, or would not, be supported over the long haul by the political leadership and public opinion. The principal "good" experience—the Persian Gulf war—confirmed the professional military's preference for the use of force to accomplish assigned missions quickly with the fewest possible U.S. casualties. So far, the Haitian and Bosnian operations have followed this model.

The tandem requirements for political support and adequate resources increased the Pentagon's cautiousness for taking on assignments it might consider marginal to U.S. vital interests. The requirement for adequate military resources to meet other contingencies simultaneously also tipped the balance against the use of force. First, the larger the force deemed necessary for the operation, the greater the cost and also the less likely that it would receive congressional support. Second, the extent to which U.S. military capabilities have been reduced in the post-cold-war period has made the military more cautious than ever about committing forces unless absolutely necessary. Can the United States afford to make substantial contributions to UN peace operations and still retain sufficient capabilities in the event U.S. interests are in jeopardy?

It is noteworthy that some of the situations examined earlier in this study did not appear easily susceptible to solutions employing U.S. combat forces. Professional military officers and expert analysts questioned the military feasibility of enforcing peace in Bosnia, supporting nation building in Somalia and combating nuclear proliferation in North Korea. Serious doubts among military professionals about whether or not specific foreign policy goals can be accomplished through the use of military force naturally inspires caution among policymakers.

More recently, however, U.S. professional military leaders appear to have accepted the principle that changing times require a more flexible approach. The former chairman of the Joint Chiefs of Staff, Gen. John M. Shalikashvili, has emphasized the importance of dealing with low-level conflicts, and he strongly supported President Clinton's decision to send troops to Haiti and Bosnia. The Army chief of staff, Gen. Dennis J.

Reimer, concurs: "The pattern of international conflict in the post-cold-war environment requires military forces to do more than just fight high-intensity conflicts."

U.S. military leaders still voice caution, however, concerning nontraditional missions and want a clear definition of their goals before they take on a specific task. But a more-permissive attitude toward peace operations among military leaders has been a key element in President Clinton's ability to use U.S. forces in support of American foreign policy goals since 1994.

Domestic Preoccupations

U.S. behavior has also been influenced by the belief that the nation neglected and deferred a variety of domestic problems during the cold war in order to sustain high levels of defense spending. The process of adjusting spending priorities actually began in the mid-1980s, as the cold war eased, when Congress passed the Gramm-Rudman-Hollings deficit-reduction act. That act gave priority to gaining control over the federal budget deficit, and it placed limits on both domestic and defense spending.

Before the cold war came to an end, experts and officials had debated whether or not the United States could afford to maintain its global role. Historian Paul Kennedy of Yale University argued that the United States would have to cut back on its international commitments or face inevitable economic "decline." Until the late 1980s, this debate remained somewhat academic: as long as a Soviet threat existed, most policymakers judged that the United States could not give up its global leadership role. They focused their attention on convincing allies to pick up more of the financial burden of maintaining international stability. Only when it became apparent in the early 1990s that the Soviet threat was gone did the nation begin to expect that a "peace dividend" could be allocated to the domestic agenda.

Candidate Clinton, in his first presidential campaign in 1992, recognized and greatly benefited from this shift in popular perceptions and priorities. "It's the economy, stupid" was the rallying cry, and concern for domestic problems was a hallmark of the campaign. President Bush's campaign managers, recognizing that their candidate was perceived as a competent foreign policy manager who was uninterested in domestic issues, attempted to change the President's image. But this endeavor was to no avail.

President Clinton's Approach

President Clinton apparently followed what he saw as the 1992 electoral message. If the United States were to bear the brunt of global burdens, as it had throughout the cold war and, more recently, in the response to the Iraqi invasion of Kuwait, the Clinton Administration could not devote its greatest efforts to domestic issues. President Clinton remained consistent with campaign positions and public opinion and did not reject an internationalist role for the United States, but he looked for ways to maintain it at reduced cost.

The President and his advisers' first solution was to rely more heavily on international cooperation, particularly on the UN, to deal with security challenges that did not directly threaten vital U.S. interests. In the post-Soviet world, this would include most of the likely disruptions of the peace. As noted, President Clinton initiated a study of U.S. peacekeeping policy (then called Presidential Review Document 13) to lay out a multilateral strategy for global security challenges. When it appeared that a policy of "assertive multilateralism" could not be sustained in Congress and in U.S. public opinion, the Administration adjusted its approach to accommodate the existing consensus.

Clinton and his key advisers also appeared anxious to avoid the fate that had befallen President Lyndon B. Johnson (1963–69), whose goal of a "Great Society" domestic presidency was undermined by the political and economic costs of U.S. involvement in Vietnam. Thus, early in his first term, President Clinton made no strong efforts to build consensus in Congress or in public opinion for an interventionist U.S. approach to global security problems. He initially accepted a shrinking U.S.

role rather than risk political capital on behalf of international objectives.

In terms of the U.S. role in the world, the Administration's performance in its first 18 months contrasted sharply with that during the balance of Clinton's first term. The Clinton Administration dispatched large and powerful forces in potentially dangerous circumstances to Haiti and Bosnia and sustained the operations in spite of significant congressional skepticism. The Haitian involvement was justified in terms of hemispheric stability, democracy and humanitarian concerns. Clinton argued that the United States had to join in the Bosnia operation to ensure successful implementation of the Dayton peace accords and for the sake of NATO's credibility and U.S. leadership of the alliance.

Whether the deployments could have been sustained politically had U.S. forces suffered casualties in combat or as the result of terrorist attacks is not known. In any case, the formula for involvement in both Haiti and Bosnia was consistent with the advice of U.S. professional military leaders—use sufficient force to ensure that U.S. soldiers cannot be successfully challenged and thereby reduce the risks they run and eliminate combat casualties or hold them to a minimum.

Diminished Expectations for the UN

During the cold war, Congress and the American people generally supported the role of the UN in helping maintain peace between parties that had agreed to stop fighting. Since the end of the cold war, the international community has been challenged to develop responses to continuing conflicts and complex civil wars. Developing a consensus in the United States has been much more difficult concerning U.S. involvement in making peace between combatants as opposed to keeping peace after the warring parties have agreed to stop fighting.

As noted earlier, President Clinton had hoped to be able to shift some of the burden of enforcing international peace and stability onto the shoulders of the international community, particularly the UN. But this expectation did not take into account the UN's lack of experience in managing military operations that prove more demanding than traditional peacekeeping. The UN's record in Somalia and Bosnia seriously undermined the world body's credibility—in the United States and elsewhere—as an effective manager of military operations.

It is quite unlikely that Congress would react favorably to the President's assigning U.S. forces to a combat operation under UN command. Such a decision is within his prerogatives as commander in chief, and Congress has never successfully challenged his authority in this regard. PDD-25 nonetheless accepts such a limitation as a given. In light of the UN's recent experience and U.S. concerns, the United States is unlikely to initiate or support proposals in the near future that would give the UN significantly greater responsibility for managing military operations. Without solid U.S. support, it will be difficult, if not impossible, for the UN to develop the competence required for the coordinated use of military capabilities to make or enforce the peace.

Congressional Qualms

Congress has consistently demonstrated its skepticism about the need for U.S. forces on the front line in a world that currently poses few direct threats to U.S. vital interests. The congressional reaction to American casualties in Somalia in particular played a direct role in the U.S. decision to withdraw from the international peace operation there. With regard to Bosnia, most members were reluctant to support deployment of U.S. ground forces even after a peace settlement had been reached. Members of the Congressional Black Caucus argued for U.S. military intervention in Haiti, but other members cautioned against such a move.

Congress therefore expresses the same appreciation of political costs and benefits that is reflected in the Administration's actions. Members of Congress, for the most part, are not willing to advocate the use of U.S. military force in potentially dangerous circumstances at a time when there is no consensus on international goals. This is particularly true when the Administration assesses that the domestic political cost of international leadership is greater than the potential benefit.

The Bottom Line

These factors combine to produce strong U.S. reluctance to intervene militarily in cases where U.S. vital interests are not threatened and U.S. troops could suffer casualties, or where the financial costs of involvement would be substantial. These considerations also lead some analysts to look askance at U.S. overseas involvement in general and to question the potential costs of even diplomatic activism. Such attitudes can be seen as part of a healthy questioning of commitments, a process that political leaders owe to their constituents. However, it is also clear that the United States has no choice but to play an important role in the world. Even from the most narrow perspective, the fate of the United States appears inextricably linked to an increasingly interdependent world. The American people recognize this in their support for a continuing U.S. leadership role and their willingness to share U.S. global leadership burdens with other nations demonstrates their understanding of the limits of U.S. resources. Perhaps it is on this foundation that the Clinton Administration can begin to build a new consensus on the U.S. role in the world for the twenty-first century.

5

Foreign Policy Bridge to the Twenty-first Century

P RESIDENT CLINTON suggested during the 1996 election campaign that the United States was the "indispensable power" in the international system. Some foreign observers might resent or even disagree with such a generalization, but, in many respects, it does capture one of the important realities of the contemporary international system. The system does not work particularly well if the United States does not play a leading, or at least a constructive, role. Perhaps the most telling evidence so far has been the situation in Bosnia. With the United States playing a halfhearted political and military role in the international community's attempt to deal with that country's civil war, the conflict continued, civilian casualties mounted and international peacekeeping forces were, in some cases, humiliated by the contending forces. In 1995, when the United States applied the full force of its diplomacy to the conflict, the parties came to the table in Dayton and signed a peace agreement. The U.S.– NATO enforcement effort has kept the peace and bought time for a political settlement and economic rehabilitation.

Yet the foundation for the "indispensable" U.S. role remains shaky and perhaps unreliable. The President was not able to win congressional endorsement of the mission in Bosnia; members simply expressed their support for the U.S. forces that were being sent there. Now that the U.S. military presence in Bosnia has been extended by 18 months, the main interest of many in Congress is ensuring that all U.S. forces are out of Bosnia by mid-1998, as the Administration has promised.

It is possible to argue that the United States has, through its actions, already begun to define its emerging role in the world. In spite of the inconsistencies of policy and direction seen in the late Bush and early Clinton years, the United States has managed to pass through the valley of isolationism and unilateralism toward a more appropriate policy. According to this perspective, that policy cannot be defined in "bumper sticker" slogans, but neither is it simply an inarticulate "muddling through." This argument has appeal because the nation may not be able to find a slogan or level of consensus for a twenty-first century foreign policy that provides as much coherence as containment did during the cold war. But in a democracy, political leadership cannot escape the responsibility to provide reasons for commitments and explanations for the costs of policies.

Meanwhile, a major foreign policy issue looms on the horizon that could well force the pace of the debate. At a NATO summit meeting in Madrid, Spain, on July 8-9, 1997, the United States and its fellow members invited the Czech Republic, Hungary and Poland to begin the process of joining the alliance. Once negotiations with the invited countries have successfully concluded, the U.S. Senate will be asked to give its advice and consent to the accession of the new members. Ratification requires two thirds of the Senate to vote in the affirmative.

One of the arguments made against inviting new East European democracies to join NATO has been that the U.S.

Congress would be unwilling to take on additional defense obligations. Article 5 of NATO's founding treaty states that "the parties agree that an armed attack against one or more of them…shall be considered an attack against them all, and consequently they agree that, if such an armed attack occurs, each of them…will assist the party or parties so attacked by taking forthwith…such action as it deems necessary, *including the use of armed force*, to restore and maintain the security of the North Atlantic area (emphasis added)."

Whether or not the Senate will approve accession of candidates to the treaty, of course, is unknown. But the decision already has engendered a debate that addresses the major questions asked at the beginning of this study. Does enlargement protect vital U.S. interests and promote important U.S. objectives in the world? How does the decision affect the values underlying U.S. foreign policy? Are the costs of NATO enlargement reasonable and affordable and will allies pay a large enough share? Is the United States making a commitment that could put U.S. lives at risk, or is it on a course that will make war in Europe less likely?

The process of enlarging NATO is likely to require that the Administration build a national consensus regarding the U.S. role in the world and, in the process, demonstrate that enlargement is justified or even required by that role. This is a task that, in order to be successful, requires the political commitment and active involvement of the President. Nobody else— not even a talented and activist secretary of state like Madeleine Albright or the legislatively experienced new secretary of defense, William S. Cohen, or leaders in Congress—can substitute for presidential leadership.

Divergent Prescriptions: Hegemony vs. Isolationism

The effort to define U.S. interests is well under way. Leading U.S. foreign policy journals and newspapers have published dozens of excellent articles by America's best foreign and defense policy thinkers. These experts have sought to describe the principal characteristics of the emerging international system and U.S. interests in that system, and they have suggested policy postures and approaches. The debate already includes a wide range of prescriptions. On one end of the spectrum, some policy analysts have argued since the early 1990s that the United States should take advantage of its position as the only surviving superpower to maximize its influence on the rest of the world. This perspective was presented as a proposed strategy for Senator Bob Dole of Kansas, the Republican candidate for President, during the 1996 campaign by William Kristol, editor, and Robert Kagan, contributing editor, of *The Weekly Standard*. They advocated a policy of "benevolent global hegemony," an approach to the U.S. role in the world in which the United States would "enshrine" its huge lead in defense capability in a declarative defense and foreign policy strategy. Invoking memories of Presidents Theodore Roosevelt (1901–09) and Ronald Reagan (1981–89), the two conservatives argued that the main threat to the United States in the twenty-first century would be "its own weakness" and that "American hegemony is the only reliable defense against a breakdown of peace and international order." U.S. policy should therefore seek to "preserve that hegemony as far into the future as possible."

This argument inspired strong reactions and counterarguments. One historian, Ronald Steel, who argued even during the cold war for a reduced U.S. role in the world, maintained that "benevolent hegemony" presents three major problems. First, according to Steel, it focuses almost entirely on military power, while the main challenges to the United States in the twenty-first century will more likely grow out of economic quarrels, migration from poor nations to rich ones and environmental disasters. Steel asks, "Do we bring out the B-2s [stealth bombers] against viruses, terrorists or the next shipment of Toyotas?" Second, in Steel's argument, "every hegemony induces its equal and opposite reaction." According to this perspective, a U.S. effort to impose even a benevolent hegemony would inspire the formation of anti-American international coalitions. Steel's third argument is economic: a policy of hegemony is expensive and the military costs of hegemony would eventually undermine the U.S. economic base.

Whether or not Steel's critique of the benevolent-hegemony school is valid, it should be noted that the antihegemonists draw heavily on traditional American tendencies toward isolationism. Those tendencies reemerged at the end of the cold war, a reflection of the cold-war fatigue discussed earlier as well as the need to attend to domestic budgetary and social issues. They prompted foreign observers of the United States to worry whether America would adopt an isolationist stance and reduce its key contribution to international security and stability, particularly in Europe and Asia.

The unilateralism projected by the hegemonists and the isolationism that inspires a more restrained view of the U.S. international role represent the two extremes in the U.S. foreign policy debate. As is usual in a democracy, the basis for consensus lies somewhere in between. The views of most experts and officials also tend to gravitate toward a middle ground in which the United States reserves the option of acting unilaterally, when necessary, but attempts to promote international cooperation and burden-sharing whenever possible. It is on this middle ground where a new consensus on U.S. interests, values and policy goals has the best chance of being constructed.

Defining the Center: Vital Interests

During 1996, two prestigious bipartisan groups of former officials, members of Congress and leading scholars and experts submitted lists of vital interests that they believe should be the basis for U.S. foreign policy. One group, supported by Harvard University, the RAND Corporation and the Nixon Center for Peace and Freedom, called itself the Commission on America's National Interests. The second group was organized by the Center for Strategic and International Studies (CSIS), a Washington, DC, think tank. Both groups decided that the concept of U.S. vital interests needed to go well beyond simply protecting America's borders.

The Commission on America's National Interests declared,

"vital national interests are conditions that are strictly necessary to safeguard and enhance the well-being of Americans in a free and secure nation." Based on this general statement, the commission members judged that it is in the U.S. vital national interests to
•prevent, deter and reduce the threat of nuclear, biological and chemical (NBC) weapon attacks on the United States;
•prevent the emergence of a hostile major power in Europe or Asia;
•prevent the emergence of an antagonistic power on U.S. borders or in control of the seas;
•prevent the catastrophic collapse of major global systems—trade, financial, energy and environment;
•ensure the survival of U.S. allies.

In order to achieve these vital goals, the group contended that the United States would be required to demonstrate international leadership, maintain necessary military capabilities, ensure U.S. credibility (by adhering to commitments and being evenhanded in dealing with other nations) and support critical multilateral institutions (for example, NATO).

The commission participants argued that the United States needed to identify some hierarchy of interests, as they had done, to help establish priorities for the time and attention of policymakers and for the allocation of scarce resources. They strongly supported a U.S. leadership role in the world and maintained that the President and his Administration bear "the lion's share of responsibility for articulating a coherent sense of American interests around which to mobilize support."

The CSIS group, using a somewhat different methodology, arrived at conclusions that were not dissimilar from those of the Harvard-Rand-Nixon Center group. The CSIS participants also sought to determine "vital" interests of the United States. The standard applied to define the meaning of vital was interests that "are of such consequence that the United States should be prepared to promote them unilaterally by whatever means necessary." They observed that such means would only sometimes require military action.

These experts and officials organized vital interests by category. In terms of international security, they included:
- protecting the U.S. homeland, including American citizens and property overseas;
- maintaining unimpeded access to key geographic areas and critical economic resources;
- ensuring the viability and inclusiveness of the evolving international system.

The CSIS group cited the following vital interests of the United States in Asia: preventing domination of the region by an adversarial power; providing security on the Korean peninsula; ensuring commercial, political and military access to and through Asia; and containing nuclear weapons and missile technology.

Concerning Europe, with particular regard to Russia, the group said that the United States had vital interests in preventing domination of the region by an adversarial power; controlling and reducing Russia's nuclear arsenal; and preventing threats to Europe, Asia and the Persian Gulf in the event of a resurgent and militant Russia.

The group also identified several vital interests in the Middle East. They include maintaining peace and stability in the Persian Gulf and the availability of oil and gas resources for export, ensuring Israel's survival as a nation-state and the security of Egypt, Saudi Arabia and Jordan, and developing coordinated, more effective responses to Middle East terrorism.

The CSIS group echoed the commission's call for "strong and assertive U.S. leadership in international affairs." Effective leadership, according to the group, will necessitate a better explanation of policy goals in terms of U.S. principles, values and interests. Bipartisan approaches, when possible, will strengthen U.S. leadership, particularly when the White House is controlled by one party and Congress by the other. And, the group noted, the United States in the future will be able to contend with very few of the world's problems on its own. A common understanding of solutions to international challenges with other nations will be absolutely critical.

The lists produced by the two study groups suggest that the country may be moving toward a broader concept of U.S. vital interests than was prevalent in the early 1990s. Given the fact that public opinion generally accepts an affordable U.S. world leadership role, maybe the United States is beginning to emerge from the escapist attitude that characterized U.S. politics and decisionmaking through the early to mid-1990s.

Values

The United States always has been and most likely always will be an "ideological power." From the first days of the Republic, Americans have believed that their country stood for something. This belief has influenced the U.S. approach to foreign policy. It frustrates and sometimes even angers America's friends and allies overseas, who occasionally find Americans too preachy because they impose their values on U.S. foreign policy. Some pragmatic strategists and even some of the most distinguished U.S. foreign policy officials have found the ideological component of U.S. foreign policy troubling, particularly if it prevents doing the "sensible" thing.

The value base of U.S. foreign policy represents a direct link between domestic politics and foreign policy. The difficulty is that there is no single set of values that is universally accepted as accurately representing "the American way of life." As a result, the inclination to let values affect foreign policy decisions guarantees debate and frequently division. People order their values differently. Some Americans may place a high value on controlling world population to avoid future famine and suffering and support allocating foreign aid for family planning abroad. Other Americans might oppose using tax dollars to support family planning overseas because it runs counter to their religious beliefs.

Allowing one part of the U.S. value base, or a narrow interpretation of values, to guide U.S. foreign and defense policies could be counterproductive. If policy is based on one value-oriented goal, it might overlook some important pragmatic considerations. For example, a policy toward China based solely on human rights would most likely guarantee a strongly confrontational relationship with that important power. An exceedingly narrow value base, while conducive to business, might not be sustainable in U.S. public opinion. An overly aggressive deployment of value-based policies might produce international reactions against U.S. values because other countries might fear U.S. "cultural imperialism."

Nonetheless, there are some broadly construed values that will be influential as the United States shapes its foreign policy for the twenty-first-century world. Support for democracy, individual liberty and the rule of law undoubtedly will serve as guideposts for U.S. relations with other nations. Americans are likely to continue to believe that their democracy will be more secure in a world that accepts these basic values to one degree or another. But this approach will have to be tempered by the realization that even these broad organizing principles will have varying degrees of relevance to societies with different historical experiences and cultural traditions. U.S. foreign policy in the twenty-first century will require a degree of tolerance and respect for diversity as well as advocacy of treasured American values.

Tools of the Trade

Even a consensus on interests and values still leaves avenues open for debate about the instruments of U.S. policy—a debate that is already under way. President Clinton, in his 1997 State of the Union address, identified his priorities. He called for maintaining "a strong and ready military." He asked for increased funding for weapons modernization by the year 2000. And he said that the country has to "take good care of our men and women in uniform." He went on to argue that the United States needed to "renew our commitment to America's diplomacy and pay our debts and dues to international financial institutions like the World Bank and to a reforming UN." Clinton concluded that failure of the United States to fund its diplomacy would limit U.S. influence in the world: "A farsighted America moved the world to a better place over these last 50 years….a shortsighted America will soon find its words falling on deaf ears all around the world." Most political analysts would agree with the broad outlines of the President's goals. But, as is often the case in Washington, the devil is in the details. With regard to military spending, many congressional Republicans would like to see more money spent and on somewhat different priorities. The 104th Congress added almost $7 billion to President Clinton's defense budget request for FY 1996 and $10.5 billion to the request for FY 1997.

Debate will continue about the use of U.S. military forces. Should they be reserved for major, threatening contingencies, or should they play an active role in peace operations like the current one in Bosnia? The Clinton Administration prepared a Bottom-Up Review in 1993 that concluded that U.S. forces should be designed to fight and win two major regional contingencies (such as a war in the Persian Gulf and another one in Korea) almost simultaneously. Some critics question whether U.S. forces could accomplish this objective in the future while also supporting peace operations in Bosnia and elsewhere.

So far, the Clinton Administration has emphasized readiness of forces over force modernization. The Administration's plan is to give greater attention to modernization over the next few years. Some congressional critics believe that modernization has already fallen dangerously behind. There are also debates about certain very expensive programs such as a ballistic-missile defense and fighter-aircraft modernization. Some members of Congress believe the United States should move more rapidly to develop a missile defense system to protect against threats from rogue states and terrorists. Others believe the highest priority should be to fund programs designed to protect U.S. forces in the field from missile threats. Those members who are particularly concerned about eliminating the budget deficit question whether it is necessary to spend more money on these expensive programs. (Since President Reagan initiated the Strategic Defense Initiative in 1983, some $80 billion has been spent on ballistic-missile defense and related programs.)

Meanwhile, the Clinton Administration's Quadrennial Defense Review of defense policy and posture, which touches on all these issues, was completed in May 1997 without revealing any radical changes in the U.S. defense posture or spending. As directed by Congress, an outside panel of experts will scrutinize the review. This process could provide the main focus of debate on U.S. defense policy, budget and programs in the months, and possibly years, ahead.

With regard to the tools of U.S. diplomacy, there is a growing belief in Washington that cuts in the foreign policy establishment have gone far enough. The bipartisan CSIS group, for example, argues that "in an increasingly untidy world in which Americans are reluctant to support military intervention, the U.S. Congress should be allocating additional resources to the tools of diplomacy rather than cutting them back." There undoubtedly is still room for institutional consolidation and reform, just as there is in virtually all bureaucratic structures. But the growing realization that U.S. diplomacy constitutes a tiny portion of U.S. government spending may help focus the debate more on what is needed to make the official foreign policy establishment more effective and somewhat less on what it costs.

Strategic Role of Arms Control

Arms-control policy rests at the intersection of defense and diplomacy. During the cold war, arms control became a key tool for managing the strategic relationship between the United States and the Soviet Union and their respective alliance systems. Arms control also developed along multilateral lines, producing universal agreements intended to limit proliferation of weapons of mass destruction and to stop nuclear testing. Today, there are major questions about the future of arms control, at least in the context of the U.S.-Russian relationship. The Strategic Arms Reduction Treaty (Start II), intended to yield substantial reductions in U.S. and Russian strategic nuclear weapons, languishes in the Russian parliament, where many members oppose ratification. This is in part, they claim, because of NATO's plan to enlarge. Many aspects of the original 1990 Treaty on Conventional Armed Forces in Europe (CFE), designed to stabilize weapon deployments between NATO and Warsaw Pact countries in Europe, have been overtaken by recent events. Negotiations have begun to "adjust" this treaty. Moreover, there are broad philosophical questions about the role of arms control in an evolving Western relationship with Russia. To what extent do traditional arms-control approaches tend to perpetuate the structure, if not the practice, of an adversarial relationship? Should the United States strive to replace negotiations on arms control with defense cooperation with the Russians, based on the assumption of common goals? This could lead to a degree of openness in defense planning and deployments. A beginning of such a new relationship perhaps can be seen in Russia's cooperation with the United States in the NATO-led force in Bosnia and in the goals incorporated in the Founding Act on Mutual Relations, Cooperation and Security, signed by Russia and the 16 members of NATO in Paris, France, on May 27, 1997.

Both a strong defense and effective diplomacy depend on U.S. decisionmakers having access to the best possible intelligence. The U.S. intelligence community faces a continuing crisis. It is generally agreed that the United States still needs the ability to retrieve, analyze and present information to the President and senior policymakers. But with the Soviet Union gone, there appears to be no consensus on the priorities that should guide intelligence collection and production. There is even less agreement on the role that clandestine intelligence activities should play in the new international order. Maybe a clearer focus on U.S. interests, objectives and values will help shape future intelligence priorities.

Finally, the debate over the advantages and disadvantages of multilateral cooperation now seems to have found some common ground. The United States cannot count on international organizations to defend its interests. Like other nations in the international system, it must reserve the right and ability to act unilaterally when necessary to protect itself militarily, politically and economically. On the other hand, in an increasingly interdependent world, even the sole-surviving superpower cannot afford to go it alone. It would cost much more than the American people are willing to pay. In addition, U.S. influence and power are generally strengthened when U.S. goals are shared by international organizations and supported by key allies. Multilateral cooperation will most likely remain a key tool for implementing the U.S. role in the twenty-first-century world. U.S. leadership in multilateral forums such as the UN Security Council will be one of the ingredients that determines whether or not international cooperation works.

Toward a New Consensus?

At the end of the day, it appears that the United States would benefit from the development of a new consensus concerning the interests and values that the United States wishes to advance and is prepared to defend (with forces and finances). Without such a consensus, the United States will find it difficult to resume the role of a relatively reliable, predictable force in international politics. That process of forming a new consensus is not easy without a mobilizing threat. Still, a case can be made that the process may have begun.

The first Clinton Administration's initial approach to foreign policy centered on promoting U.S. economic interests and reducing costly U.S. military commitments abroad. In September 1993, the Administration added the goal of "enlarging the area of democracy" to its approach, creating a foreign policy mix that included widely shared values, economic self-interest and a proclaimed political objective. When military intervention appeared necessary to pursue major U.S. foreign policy objectives (reestablish civilian rule in Haiti and implement the peace accord in Bosnia), the Administration acted. Those interventions may have begun to validate the importance of using force when necessary on behalf of U.S. foreign policy objectives.

Still unformed, however, is a national consensus on priorities and policy instruments. If promoting democracy requires that the United States take some risks and spend money on such things as foreign aid, alliance commitments and military intervention, how should the country choose between its pocketbook and its principles? If a measure of international order is important to long-term U.S. interests, what criteria should determine if U.S. soldiers should risk their lives? An Administration option might be to develop a new statement of U.S. values, interests, goals and policy instruments. The model could be the process that led to the articulation of U.S. goals in NSC-68 at the beginning of the cold war. (NSC-68, "United States Objectives and Programs for National Security," was the product of a U.S. government review and redefinition of U.S. policies initiated in the aftermath of the first Soviet nuclear test in 1949.) Such a study could, in theory, result in a call for a neo-isolationist posture on one extreme or an active, interventionist "pax Americana" posture on the other. But it is much more likely to result in a recommendation for some form of active U.S. leadership within a multilateral context that includes effective burden-sharing with allies and requires joint leadership responsibilities.

Such a formal reevaluation process would be difficult and, perhaps initially, divisive. The deliberations could not be contained within the government bureaucracy, and the debate inevitably would spill over into the press and public discussion. Indeed, the Administration might encourage such a public debate. Those in and outside the Administration who have argued that the United States should concentrate on U.S. economic interests and retreat from global political commitments would be pitted against others who favor a robust multilateralist approach.

In the end, however, the process might yield a new compromise. This could be the foundation for a U.S. role in the world that balances the domestic and international interests and responsibilities of the world's only superpower. Such a foundation presumably would include a list of vital interests and key values that reflect post-cold-war realities and would restore flexibility to U.S. policymaking.

No private analyst, group or even Congress can substitute for executive leadership in defining the new American role in the world. If the United States is eventually to move away from its recent reticence on the world stage, the President will most likely have to lead the country in that direction. Nevertheless, Congress and the public can play important roles in the process of constructing a new consensus on U.S. interests, values and the use of force in their defense in the post-cold-war world. Moreover, leadership by the President and debate in the Congress can give the American public opportunities to judge the quality of the arguments on all sides and play a part in decisions that could have profound implications for current and future generations of Americans in the twenty-first century.

Talking It Over

A Note for Students and Discussion Groups

This issue of the HEADLINE SERIES, like its predecessors, is published for every serious reader, specialized or not, who takes an interest in the subject. Many of our readers will be in classrooms, seminars or community discussion groups. Particularly with them in mind, we present below some discussion questions—suggested as a starting point only—and references for further reading.

Discussion Questions

The United States emerged from the cold war as the only surviving superpower. What attitude toward this circumstance will serve U.S. interests best? What are the implications for other countries?

What balance should be struck between the need for the United States to protect its interests in global affairs and the generally agreed goal of reducing the budget deficit?

What are the most important U.S. interests as the twenty-first century approaches? How important is it to define those interests?

In the past, it has been generally accepted that American

democracy would be safer in a world in which more nations became democracies with free-market economies. Should a policy of promoting democratization be a major part of U.S. foreign policy? Under what conditions should the United States be willing to use force on behalf of its foreign policy goals? If the United States is unwilling to use its military forces in dangerous circumstances, how can any degree of order be maintained in the international system?

As long as the United States faces no direct challenge to its borders, should the training and equipping of U.S. forces concentrate more than in the past on preparations for "peace operations" like the one in Bosnia?

Over the last decade, the U.S. foreign policy establishment and its programs, such as foreign aid, have been deeply cut. Is the United States in danger of losing influence overseas and increasing reliance on the use of U.S. military forces, as former Secretary of State Christopher has warned?

What balance should be struck between the unilateral aspects of U.S. foreign policy and the multilateral aspects? How important is it to convince other countries to cooperate with the United States?

How important is it for the President to try to shape a new consensus on America's role in the world? Should he seek a bipartisan consensus with the Republican majority in the Congress? How important is public opinion in this regard?

Annotated Reading List

Brzezinski, Zbigniew, "Geopolitical Pivot Points." *The Washington Quarterly*, Autumn 1996. Former national security adviser summarizes his formula for U.S. foreign policy leadership.

Commission on America's National Interests, "America's

National Interests." Center for Science and International Studies, Harvard University, Cambridge, MA, July 1996. Bipartisan group identifies U.S. national interests in post-cold-war world.

"Foreign Policy into the 21st Century: The U.S. Leadership Challenge." Center for Strategic and International Studies, Washington, DC, September 1996. Bipartisan group outlines U.S. interests, values and policy approaches for 21st-century U.S. role in the world.

Haass, Richard, *Intervention: The Use of American Military Force in the Post-Cold War World*. Washington, DC, Carnegie Endowment for International Peace, 1995. Survey of U.S. approach to military intervention in post-cold-war world.

Helms, Jesse, "Saving the U.N." *Foreign Affairs*, Sept./Oct. 1996. The leading congressional critic of the UN makes his case.

Kristol, William, and Kagan, Robert, "Toward A Neo-Reaganite Foreign Policy." *Foreign Affairs*, July/Aug. 1996. Conservatives recommend a policy of benign hegemony.

Kull, Steven, and Destler, I.M., "An Emerging Consensus, A Study of American Public Attitudes on America's Role in the World." Center for International and Security Studies at the University of Maryland and its Program on International Policy Attitudes (PIPA), July 10, 1996. Public opinion experts assess attitudes toward U.S. role in the world.

Omestad, Thomas, "Foreign Policy and Campaign 96." *Foreign Policy*, Winter 1996–97. Assessment of foreign policy content of the 1996 presidential campaign.

Perry, William J., "Defense in an Age of Hope." *Foreign Affairs*, Nov./Dec. 1996. Former Secretary of Defense lays out concepts behind Clinton Administration security policy.

Steel, Ronald, *Temptations of a Superpower*. Cambridge, MA, Harvard University Press, 1995. Leading proponent of constrained U.S. role in world assesses post-cold-war U.S. interests.

Talbott, Strobe, "Democracy and the National Interest." *Foreign Affairs*, Nov./Dec. 1996. Clinton Administration foreign policy official argues that when America promotes democracy, values and interests reinforce each other.

The White House, "A National Security Strategy of Engagement and Enlargement," February 1996. Official presentation of Clinton Administration foreign policy goals

Yost, Casmir, and Locke, Mary, "U.S. Foreign Affairs Resources: Budget Cuts and Consequences." Occasional Paper, Institute for the Study of Diplomacy, Georgetown University, Washington, DC, 1996. Calls attention to cuts in spending for U.S. foreign policy agencies and programs.